How I Run My Trading Strategy Whilst Working Full Time

Craig Flint

COPYRIGHT

DEDICATION

To my darling wife Joanna who has been very patient with me through some testing times in learning how to trade.

CONTENTS

INTRODUCTION

**How I Run My Trading Strategy
Whilst Working Full Time**

By Craig Flint

- ●●●●● -

Are you considering a change of career and making the transition to become a full time trader?

Perhaps you are planning on testing the waters first and trading whilst in a full time job?

Maybe you're struggling to cope with the demands of holding down your job whilst running your automated strategy?

Whatever your situation, this book shows you how it can be done by detailing the comprehensive toolkit I use to effectively run my automated trading strategy - with minimal interruption to my working life.

Part One

BACKGROUND

I currently work full time as a qualified Finance Professional residing in the UK. For years I have had a burning desire to give up my full time occupation and commence trading for a living in order to escape the shackles of working for someone else and really start earning extreme amounts of wealth. I have a fair way to go before I realise this target however I believe that learning from my experiences to date and trading with the complete toolkit I now use will get me there eventually.

Profitable trading is a tough objective, however with the right mindset and discipline coupled with the appropriate tools, I believe it is certainly achievable for the average person.

If you already have the means and plan to give up working full time soon to begin trading then I wish you well, however if you are like me and need the security of a steady income by way of a full time job whilst learning the ropes of becoming a trader, then this book will hopefully be of significant use to you.

It can be extremely difficult to trade when at work as employers clearly don't want their staff members distracted and so many prevent access to trading platforms and websites. In addition to this, you may attend meetings on a frequent basis or may simply be too busy to spend enough time to trade effectively. This book is therefore intended to share with you my complete set-up which will hopefully save you months of trial and error, research, problem solving and frustration.

The complete toolkit I use enables me to successfully manage a full time office based job whilst discretely trading my strategy through the use of automated trading.

Whichever way your path turns on your trading journey, I'm not going to end up wishing you lots of luck. This may sound strange at first however I firmly believe luck should play very little part in your trading activity. Instead you need the right discipline, a suitable strategy, appropriate technology, and sound money management techniques to succeed.

It should be noted that this book is not intended to be used for advice. Your own circumstances will dictate what is best for you with regards to what markets or strategy to trade, which trading platform or broker to employ or how your trading may impact your working life. You trade entirely at your own risk and you should conduct your own research thoroughly before making any trading or investment decisions. Seek independent and qualified advice.

My current set-up may not be suitable for your circumstances – you may prefer a different trading platform, broker, or monitoring system.

Please note I have not profited in any way from the organisations mentioned in this book – I considered potential marketing opportunities at the outset however I decided against this so I could maintain integrity to you the reader. I do endorse these companies on a personal level however this is purely because I am happy with the services I currently receive (which of course could change). For each tool I use, other alternatives are for the most part widely available.

1.1

FINANCIAL TRADING – DO YOUR RESEARCH

This book is not a reference guide to trading. There is an abundance of informative resource on the internet and in books with in-depth explanations and advice so I will leave it up to you to do your own thorough research if you haven't done so already.

Choosing what financial instrument to trade is a very personal choice and will depend on various factors such as your own risk level, tax status and accessibility. I currently favor spread betting as I enjoy the potential tax benefits it provides but this particular financial instrument may not suit you.

If there is one recommendation I would rank very highly in terms of importance, it would be that you need to learn trading yourself and not rely on other people's knowledge, approach to trading or strategy.

It is possible for two people to run exactly the same strategy rules over a period of time with one profiting and one losing. This is because one of the traders chooses to stick rigidly to the rules no matter what whereas the other decides to deviate from the rules based on fear or greed or even impatience. Read up on the original Turtle Traders for a great real life illustration of this subject.

I don't personally believe a strategy exists that will profit in all market scenarios – even the most robust strategy will most likely have periods of losses. This is because market dynamics are always changing in varying degrees.

I think a possible key to generating serious wealth in trading is by building up an account by gradually increasing lot sizes and risking a low proportion of account equity on each trade. I'm increasingly switching my mindset to think of the number of points won or lost on each trade as opposed to the actual monetary values realised.

I have always avoided purchasing a strategy. I cannot get my mind around why someone would want to sell their touted "holy grail" strategy which promises a great fortune. Wouldn't you want to keep it secret and trade it discreetly in the knowledge you will surely become very rich if it is indeed that good?

Many commercially available off-the-shelf strategies have likely been highly optimised based on numerous technical (leading or lagging) indicators that have been shown to profit on backtested historical data. This is fairly easy – I can certainly design historically profitable strategies this way. The problem normally occurs at the point of trading the strategy for real when suddenly they don't perform so well and sometimes actually end up losing over the long term.

Historic data is just that – historic. It is made up of recorded events that have happened in the past so there is little point fine tuning a strategy to the nth degree on old data.

My early days of attempting to come up with a robust strategy included many (in hindsight, I now regard as quite pointless) computer hours of optimising indicators until a nice profit curve was found. Of course, when testing the final optimised strategy in a demo trading account, lo and behold I would make losses and see a new downward curve form on that once pretty graph.

The current strategy that I am trading live is doing absolutely fine and it does not include any indicators. Not a single one. It is instead based on prices alone and follows the medium term trends of my chosen markets.

1.2

SOME OF MY EARLY EXPERIENCES OF TRADING

Within a few minutes of finishing my first draft of this book's introduction, I received an email alert confirming that my automated trading strategy had closed a losing trade on the DAX index to the tune of around 100 points.

It's a timely reminder of how trading can be mentally tough – especially when encountering long losing streaks which can be very tough to trade through as doubts about your tried and trusted strategy creep in as it starts looking decidedly unreliable.

I have been trading various markets for around 4 years now and have gone through the mill a bit along the way. I remember the very first day I came upon the idea of trading – I was sitting at my desk when working for one of the biggest global computer manufacturers thinking to myself how I could possibly avoid having to work for someone else for the rest of my working life. I started searching on Google for ways of making money and trading caught my eye due to the potential high earnings and the sheer accessibility.

I freely admit I was sucked in by reading all of the success stories out there. Watching films such as Wall Street only served to make the allure of trading stronger.

At first I very naively thought trading would be a relatively easy way to supplement my income. I'm very comfortable working with numbers and I believed someone educated with a professional qualification would most likely do better than average from day one. At the time, I clearly had no idea of how much experience I would personally need to get to where I am today.

I remember placing my very first live spread bet trades on the work laptop whilst talking to my boss when we were in an informal meeting! After just a few minutes of playing around with a demo account, I thought I was ready to dip my toes into the trading waters. I was literally making complete guesses (by simply viewing bars on a live chart) as to the direction of where the FTSE index was going and I placed my long or short trades without any thought to stop losses. Luckily I didn't lose too much with my £1 stakes but a sharp move whilst not paying attention could have easily lost me over a £100. Markets can move very quickly so always use money management techniques to limit your downside risk.

I've traded various markets such as indices, FOREX, and commodities by trading various instruments including spread bets, CFD's, and futures. I've sampled short term day trading, long term trading over a period of weeks and somewhere in between which is where my current strategy sits. I've traded with more than 10 different brokers – each with varying degrees of system reliability and customer support. Some brokers I've used were based overseas although I've found this is much more risky due to time differences affecting customer and technical support and also potential latency issues when completing orders.

I've used many trading platforms, ranging from internet based, downloaded bespoke broker packages to fully fledged trading platforms such as Ninja Trader, IQ Trader, and Metatrader 4.

Now on to some of my experiences:

<u>Case 1</u> - A freezing spread bet platform

After determining that I could access a particular online trading platform on the office computer (a rarity due to company firewall restrictions), I decided to try out spread betting from the office. I didn't have a particular plan for my trade entry and exits so my approach was totally flawed from the start but I was keen to get started in my new "trading career". A problem that I hadn't considered was a totally unreliable platform with a major freezing problem which is clearly a major issue when you need to close a position quickly. The general customer support from the company was terrible which when coupled with the platform problems provided for an unusable set-up.

This did give me valuable experience though as it quickly taught me some of the dangers of both how I was trading and who I was trading with. I promptly withdrew my funds and closed the account.

What did I learn from this experience? *Trading with no clear plan for entry and exit is fraught with danger and will likely ruin a trading account. It is extremely hard to work full time and be able to concentrate on implementing trades at the same time. I also learned how important it is to thoroughly test a platform before live trading and have an immediate plan of action if problems occur – e.g. know who to contact in an emergency if a trade needs closing and you're unable to do so. This experience was also a stark warning that broker promises on websites are to be taken with a pinch of salt as live performance can differ remarkably.*

<u>Case 2</u> – Pairs trading loss

A few months into trading, I researched and gained interest in the world of pairs trading - for example going long the FTSE and simultaneously shorting the DOW. I concentrated on the fact that this can be a lower risk strategy and so began trading on my predetermined signal criteria.

One problem was that I didn't have an exit strategy at all. The trade was £2 per point on the FTSE and £1 on the DOW and I was targeting something like a £20 profit. Things quickly turned against me though and there I was one evening watching the screen and seeing my losses get worse and worse until they breached £100.

I kept thinking that the market would "correct" and be kind to me and go back in my favour. This situation evidently culminated in a very poor risk/reward ratio – I was trying to make around £20 but was risking more than £100. Clearly this is totally unsustainable and will likely blow an account in no time. When I finally closed the trade out of despair with a loss of around £60, I was pretty stressed out. This ruined my evening and made me severely doubt whether trading was a good occupation to be getting into.

What did I learn from this experience? *Never assume the market will act in a forgiving fashion and "correct" back to where you want it to go. As in my experience with the freezing platform, entering a trade without a proper exit plan is very risky. Losses can quickly get out of hand – imagine if I'd been trading £10 or £100 per point. Ending up completely stressed is not a state of mind to be trading in – it* *will most likely lead to very poor decisions and may end up proving costly both in terms of finances and health.*

Case 3 – Trading £10 a point futures using my home P.C when at work!

After several months of trying to trade manually, I started reading up on the advantages of using an automated trading system. This interest was borne out of many frustrating occasions of trying to work full time and manually manage my trades at the same time.

I opened an account with an overseas futures broker and chose the IQ Trader platform as it offered an extremely easy way to kick start my automated trading by way of a drag and drop interface to build a strategy.

As I couldn't download the platform at work (again due to company firewall restrictions) I made the rather silly decision to try and automatically trade from my home computer which I left switched on all day. So that I could monitor things, I used a remote desktop solution so that I could access and interact with my home computer from work.

My first trade opened according to my strategy at the minimum possible trade size of £10 per point on a FTSE index futures contract.

All seemed well until I noticed that my floating profit figure hadn't changed in a while which was in fact due to a dropped connection. My remote desktop session suggested it was either my home computer or the IQ Trader platform had frozen.

In a panic, I phoned my broker to check the state of my open position. Luckily it was still in profit so I left it open as I was adamant about sticking with my exit rules in my strategy. Unfortunately, the tide turned against me and my trade went into a loss making situation. The main problem I had was that I couldn't tell how loss making it was and whether IQ Trader would automatically close it correctly.

In the end I had to close it manually for a relatively small loss. This was a very stressful experience as whilst trying to do my full time job, I was frantically trying to manage an open position using a very poor system set-up.

What did I learn from this experience? Trying to use a home computer remotely for trading is risky and I would not encourage it. An incident of my system, trading platform, or home internet connection going down without appropriate backup facilities (such as power for my desktop computer in case of an outage) can cause major problems when running a trading strategy and losses can quickly mount when trading larger lot sizes. Aside from the technical aspects of opening and closing trades, it can be a stressful time when working full time.

Another issue was my lack of forward testing the platform – this is essential to understand the sheer reliability and also the implications to your trading if the platform or connection fails.

Part Two

**HOW I RUN MY TRADING STRATEGY
WHILST WORKING FULL TIME**

2.1

INTRODUCTION TO MY EXISTING SET-UP

You may be wondering why I chose the fly as the picture for this book's cover. One of my hobbies is macro photography and I have grown to appreciate the fine details when studying a subject up close. I like to think of my trading toolkit in the same manner – the devil is in the detail when it comes to running an automated solution as smoothly as possible.

As you may realise from reading some of my past experiences earlier, after months and months of trying different platforms and remote ways of managing my trades whilst at work, it became apparent that my approach just wasn't working for me. I was missing entry and exit signals when trading manually, system downtime events were proving costly, and it was proving too challenging emotionally. I needed to find and adopt a better way of systematically running my strategy. And I wanted to do this discretely so my full time job was unaffected.

This section details all of the tools I currently use to effectively run my trading strategy automatically with minimal disruption to my full time job.

In my opinion, a reliable monitoring system is as important as the trading platform itself being run to execute the trades.   My chosen monitoring structure notifies me of two key aspects – i). actual trading activities and ii). incidents of system downtime.

2.2

MY STRATEGY AND CHOSEN MARKETS

I have absolute faith in my current strategy which is a trend following system that trades once or twice a week at the most. It is simple, includes no technical indicators and I have been trading it for quite a while now. My initial forward testing and now my live trading results closely match my backtest results for the same period so I believe in the historical indications of it being profitable over the long term.

I trade both the FTSE and DAX indices in unison (independently and not in a pairs set-up) and have modelled how I intend to grow my account gradually by using appropriate position sizing practices.

I'm not going to share the specifics of my strategy details as not only is it the result of much hard work, I also believe this will be a waste of time for most people. I firmly believe a trader has to find his own strategy rules that accommodate his or her levels of risk, time available, degree of patience and so on.

I find my strategy suits me personally as it has a potentially very good risk/reward ratio, trades frequently enough to be able to grow my account without having to wait decades for a very high return and doesn't trade too often which could otherwise prove too distracting when working my full time job.

My strategy may not end up making me the fortune I'm aiming for and as I said I won't be revealing all the details but this book isn't about sharing strategies – it is instead a guide on the tools I use to actually run my strategy whilst working full time.

2.3

METATRADER 4 PLATFORM (MT4)

To be able to run my strategy automatically (i.e. to execute the buy and sell opening and closing orders based on predefined signals and without my manual intervention) I need to use a trading platform that offers automated trading.

I personally favor the use of MT4 as I find it easy to use, it runs smoothly and reliably and my broker offers the markets I wish to trade via this particular platform. I have used MT4 for a number of years now and can therefore vouch for its fast speed and reliability over a long period of time.

There are countless online resources and forums that have enabled me to build up a relatively quick understanding of how to trade automatically by using MT4's "Expert Advisors" – these are covered in the next chapter.

If you favor technical trading, it is also possible to create your own custom indicators and trade with them directly on charts within MT4.

Another aspect of the MT4 platform I like is the fact that it is continually updated to ensure any system bugs and inefficiencies are ironed out.

2.4

AUTOMATED TRADING WITH EXPERT ADVISORS

An Expert Advisor consists of a set of instructions written in MQL4 which is a programming language. When written correctly, the complete Expert Advisor can be attached to a chart in MT4 and used to monitor every tick for your desired entry and exit criterion.

To illustrate, suppose you want to enter a sell trade on the GBP/USD market when the price breaches a certain level such as a two week low. An Expert Advisor can be coded to watch the GBP/USD market for this scenario and send a sell order to the broker accordingly. You would simply drag and drop the completed Expert Advisor to the GBP/USD chart and ensure automatic trading is switched on.

It must be noted that I am not a programmer - not even close. I have instead built up my limited knowledge of Expert Advisor coding from lots of research and using extracts from freely available Expert Advisor's out there. This approach does have it's drawbacks as when something doesn't work as it should, it can be very hard to figure out how to fix it. Errors can occur when even a single bracket or brace is missing or in the wrong place. It can also be a very long process to get the final fully functioning coded result – the length of time will mainly depend on how complex your strategy rules are and how comfortable you are working with code.

I have come across and used a couple of web based tools that allow you to devise the code of your Expert Advisor simply by choosing the criteria in a series of drop down menus. This is at the very least a helpful place to start.

If you have a very complicated and advanced strategy, you may opt to pay a developer to code it for you or you may decide to purchase an advanced software package that creates the coding for you.

Once you have completed your Expert Advisor, you can then start backtesting it using historical data within MT4's built-in Strategy Tester.

Before committing your Expert Advisor to live trading, you should contemplate thoroughly forward testing it on a demo account to ensure it runs as you expect and is bug free. It is important to note that using a demo account may not be representative of how actual trades will transact in a live account.

2.5

RUNNING MY STRATEGY ON A VIRTUAL PRIVATE SERVER (VPS)

A major dilemma I had when starting out was with which computer to trade with. Using my home computer remotely when in the office proved way too perilous due to possible power outages or dropped internet connections. Also the office firewalls proved too restrictive. In addition, I was sometimes away from both my home and the office so I found it impossible to carefully monitor and run my strategy throughout the trading day.

The solution I have found to be the most effective for me is to run my MT4 terminal on a Virtual Private Server (VPS). If you choose a solid provider with excellent reliability and uptime, you can then rely on their high quality servers and resources to ensure your trading time is maximised and with a bit of fortune problem free. Using a VPS for trading can be very straightforward. I use a Windows version and after undertaking the easy account set-up process with my provider, it was simply a case of downloading the MT4 software so I could begin putting together my automated strategy set-up.

I currently use Cloud Next's VPS offering in the UK which I have found to be very reliable and their support is very good. There are of course numerous alternatives out there with some VPS packages even being marketed specifically for trading purposes.

If MT4 is your preferred trading platform, I would always recommend choosing a Windows version VPS and not (a typically cheaper) Linux version. Although I cannot confirm for sure, I have read that MT4 doesn't run on the Linux platform and even if you can complete the installation, it can be problematic to set up and may not run smoothly over time.

I was fortunately able to fully trial my VPS before committing to a monthly contract which is a great way to assess whether the provider's solution will work for you at zero expense.

With regards to the location of your VPS, I always deem it best to go for one that physically resides in the same country as your broker's systems to minimise latency however it is also important to consider the working hours of their telephone or online support in the case of problems e.g. if your VPS unexpectedly goes offline.

As in the case of forward testing your strategy on your chosen trading platform, consider forward testing the trading platform itself (using a demo account) on your new VPS when initially set-up.

This is to make sure all systems operate together correctly.

It is worth noting that I include MT4 in the Startup menu of Windows – this is so that in the event of my VPS inadvertently going down and restarting, my MT4 terminal can restart automatically. Details like this ensure my automatic trading runs as smoothly as possible with absolutely minimal downtime.

2.6

KEEPING MY VPS RUNNING SMOOTHLY

To ensure my VPS continues to run smoothly, I also restart my server every morning before the trading day starts. I have set up a scheduled task in Windows to run this restart automatically for me.

If you would like to schedule a restart of your VPS, I suggest you search online for **"schedule vps shutdown task"** as I found this particular search term yielded results to get me started. In short, you will be scheduling the program **'c:/windows/system32/shutdown.exe'** to run but with the addition of some extra parameters that will ensure the restart process kicks off immediately afterwards.

It is probably not necessary to perform a restart on a daily basis, but I have read that a VPS can become unstable is left running constantly for too long and my general working experience of Windows does support this theory.

I believe my daily restart is prudent as an unstable system could adversely affect the trading platform session which might ultimately interrupt the running of the strategy or cause problems when orders are being filled.

It is normally possible to schedule the VPS restart to run automatically like in my set-up so this could be a great option for someone who may be frequently away or who wants to minimise regular manual maintenance tasks.

2.7

VPS AUTO LOGON AFTER RESTART

Please note that the feature described below can pose a security risk.

When my VPS routinely and automatically restarts (or recovers from an unexpected problem), I consider it essential for the system to automatically log in to Windows. Otherwise my MT4 terminal cannot open and trading will be halted.

I believe there are multiple ways of doing this but the method I have selected is to update my registry file for this process to take place. Updating a registry can be a very risky thing to do if you don't know what you're doing so please research this area well before making any changes. One false move could render your system unstable or unusable. Also ensure that you have made all the necessary back-ups (including registry file) before starting.

The registry entry keys I use in my Windows 2008 VPS are as follows:-

1. AutoAdminLogon (the value should equal **1**)

2. DefaultUserName (the value should equal your administrator logon name)

3. DefaultPassword (the value should equal your administrator's logon password)

These entry keys are found in the following registry subkey:-

HKEY_LOCAL_MACHINE\SOFTWARE\Microsoft\ Windows NT\CurrentVersion\Winlogon

Please note that if no DefaultPassword string is specified, Windows automatically changes the value of the AutoAdminLogon key from **1** (true) to **0** (false), which disables the AutoAdminLogon feature.

2.8

DAILY RESTART OF THE MT4 SESSION USING SCHEDULED EVENTS

As I now automatically restart my VPS each morning (as described earlier), I no longer use the following routine however I have still included the details as you may prefer to manually restart your VPS, schedule on a less frequent basis or not at all.

This section may or may not actually apply to you if you use MT4 as your trading platform. One thing I found however when trading live continually on my VPS were occasions of some market symbols being greyed out in MT4's 'Market Watch' window for varying periods of time. When this happened, trades were not able to be executed and filled.

This was clearly a severe problem for my automated trading as it meant a huge risk of leaving a losing position open for longer than my exit rules stated. It also meant missed opening trades. After extensive investigations of trying to find the cause proved futile, I eventually stumbled upon my resolution which was to simply close and reopen my MT4 session each morning before the start of trading.

This action had the effect of refreshing the system and I didn't experience the greying out problem again. To this day, I'm still not sure where the problem actually stems from but this solution worked for me.

To ensure I carried out both the close and reopen actions daily and outside of my trading window (i.e. when the markets I trade are closed so my automated trading is not affected), I used two simple Windows scripts that were scheduled to run each morning on my VPS.

I will leave it up to you to figure out if you need them and how to schedule these scripts using the Windows scheduler tool to run them automatically. The scripts I used in my Windows Server 2008 VPS were as follows:

Closing MT4 script (copy and paste into Notepad and save as a .bat file, then schedule for automatic running):-

taskkill /im terminal.exe

<u>Opening MT4 script</u> (copy and paste into Notepad and save as a .bat file, then schedule for automatic running):-

```
rem *** This script starts the terminal after
waiting 5 seconds ***
rem *** Simply enter the directory to your
terminal.exe below***
ping localhost -n 5
start "1" "C:\Program Files\Your directory
here\terminal.exe"
exit
```

As you can see, I included two remarks in the script – this is merely a helpful reminder of how to change the code if need be.

You use these scripts entirely at your own risk. If you do decide to try them out, I recommend fully testing them when the markets are closed or live trading is switched off.

2.9

EMAIL ALERTS FOR OPENING AND CLOSING TRADES

When I'm at work, I occasionally look online to see how the markets are trading as this keeps me abreast on whether a trade signal in my strategy is likely to trigger any time soon. However it is not practical for me to watch the markets constantly whilst working. So how do I know when a trade signal does occur?

So that I am informed when a trade is triggered (either opening or closing), I use the email alert functionality in MT4. As soon as possible after I receive the alert, I do like to access my VPS to make sure the trade was filled correctly and everything is still functioning properly. I think it is wrong to assume everything is well as your email alert may have been sent but a problem may have occurred at the point of order filling.

As I use a Smartphone, I am able to use push email to effectively receive the alerts in near real time. In addition to opening and closing alerts, my Expert Advisor is coded so that I also receive emails if there has been a problem e.g. the trade could not be filled as the market was temporarily closed for trading.

2.10

REMOTE ACCESS TO MY VPS AT WORK

I want to be able to periodically check everything is running smoothly (especially when a position is open) which is where remote access on my Smartphone comes in. I own a Blackberry (without a touch screen) and have found that the TSMobiles application from SHAPE Services to be the most effective for me however I know there are alternatives available. As this is a tool that sends and receives data, sufficient network coverage where you need to remotely access your VPS the most is essential.

It can be a bit of a challenge working with the VPS's desktop on such a small screen however I use this for simple monitoring and viewing most of the time so it's not an issue for me. The TSMobiles application does include a zoom function to make viewing that much easier. The main advantage of using my phone is the fact that I can conspicuously and quickly log into my VPS to check things – whether it's at my desk, in a meeting, or even stuck in a traffic jam!

To ensure I don't have duplicate sessions open (which would mean possible duplicate trade activity), I always remotely access my VPS on a 'Console' session whether I'm using my Smartphone, my home p.c. or my tablet computer. This is an extremely important aspect to be fully understood when using any kind of remote session to view your VPS.

2.11

REMOTE ACCESS TO MY VPS AT HOME

At home I use a desktop computer which runs Windows XP. I find the most straightforward method of setting up, viewing and changing anything in my VPS is to use a Remote Desktop Connection (RDC) which is a Windows tool usually found in Accessories from the Start menu. I have a shortcut to the RDC on my computer desktop and it takes a few seconds to connect each time.

As mentioned in the last chapter, I always access my VPS using a 'Console' session to avoid duplicate sessions – this was an option I had to choose when initially setting up my RDC.

I also have an iPad tablet computer and I find it very convenient to be able to access my VPS on this as my main computer may be switched off or I may be away from home. A great application I have found is WyseCloud which serves me very well. It was extremely easy to set up and once connected, my VPS is a doddle to use. I now use my iPad each morning when having breakfast so that I can make sure everything is running as it should be in readiness for the new trading day.

2.12

MONITORING FOR DOWNTIME OF MY VPS

My current chosen VPS package doesn't include any functionality to alert me if my VPS goes down so it was up to me to look for a third party solution for downtime monitoring.

If my VPS provider has some kind of technical problem and my server shuts down, this will clearly also close down my MT4 trading terminal and trading will freeze. If a problem does occur, I need to know ASAP so that I can contact the support team and once back up and running again, make sure my trading session resumes correctly.

So that I am notified if my VPS does go down, I use a monitoring service provided by a company called Monitis. My purchased package includes three different Monitis server locations that all attempt to contact my VPS every minute of the day. I chose the UK, Germany, and the Netherlands but there are a multitude of location choices around the globe. If all three of my chosen locations report a failure to contact my VPS (thereby indicating my VPS if offline), I will receive an email alert. I have also purchased a monthly SMS alerts package to help notify me as a back-up just in case my push email on my Smartphone experiences a problem or delay.

As well as receiving the problem alerts, I have also chosen to receive the resolution alerts to tell me when my VPS is back online.

For both the problem and resolution alerts, I have elected to only receive one per instance – otherwise, I could be bombarded with scores of alerts before the problem has been resolved.

Note that I have set up an exception period for receiving alerts of around 15 minutes which corresponds to the time slot in which my VPS is scheduled to automatically restart each morning. This prevents any unnecessary alerts being sent and a further benefit of this filter is to avoid needlessly using up my SMS alert allowance where there is a monthly limit.

2.13

MONITORING FOR MT4 DISCONNECTIONS TO MY BROKER

Although my VPS may well be running smoothly, the MT4 terminal session could encounter a sudden disconnection to my broker so I find it crucial to use another monitoring tool to check for this.

I use 'MT4 Auto-restart' which is a free tool provided by a company called MT4i. The tool is actually an Expert Advisor which I attach to a chart and it detects problems with the MT4 terminal's connection to my broker by way of constantly monitoring.

In the settings menu, I simply set the number of seconds of downtime required to trigger an email alert to be sent to me. Once the connection to the broker has been restored, I receive another email alert confirming all is well again. This tool can also be set to automatically restart the MT4 terminal which MT4i claims is usually enough to clear any connection problem.

MT4i offer a comprehensive instruction manual to accompany this tool which is well written and clearly laid out. I found this essential reading as I learnt that if you want to change any parameters in the tool (e.g. number of seconds before alerts are sent), you must first reattach the Expert Advisor to the chart and not just amend the properties as you usually would with a normal Expert Advisor.

Part Three

PREPARING MY MT4 STRATEGY

3.1

CHOOSING MY BROKER

It may sound obvious but I consider an extremely important aspect of my trading is using a broker I can rely on and trust will do a good job in executing my orders. When considering which broker to use, I always first test them out by fully utilising their demo account to get a feel of their system. A constantly failing demo system can provide warning signs of potentially poor performing live systems. I will also try out the customer support and choose a broker who offers either online or (preferably) telephone support that covers the trading period of the markets I have selected to trade.

I live in the UK and always opt for an FSA regulated company so that I can rest assured that my funds are protected and I have someone to go to in the event of a major complaint if that should ever arise.

I believe your intended trading frequency should play a part in choosing a suitable broker. For example some firms may use suitable systems (e.g. for hedging customer's positions) to allow high frequency trading such as scalping whereas some may prohibit such practices.

I also carefully consider which markets and trading platforms the broker offers and whether the spreads on offer are fixed or variable.

I haven't yet come across a broker who will provide free comprehensive support for automated tools such as MT4's Expert Advisors. When using these, you're on your own and you use them entirely at your own risk. If something goes wrong with your automated trading due to a problem with your code or system set-up, don't expect your broker to compensate you for any lost equity.

3.2

BACKTESTING – USEFULNESS AND WEAKNESSES

Once I have completed an Expert Advisor, I backtest it on historical data to get a rough idea on how it has performed in the past. Backtest results indicate approximate profiles for profitability, equity drawdown, win percentages and profit factor (the ratio of gross profit to gross loss – the higher the ratio, the better).

However I always keep in mind that this is only useful to a point – the results are based on assumed events that have happened in the past and shouldn't be relied upon as an extremely accurate account. Backtest results make the assumption that every order was filled without any problems or delay and with no slippage on price. Also be aware that historic data may include errors or gaps which can skew results.

When comparing actual results to backtest results over the same period, I've found those strategies using longer time period charts (e.g. using daily bars) can be much more closely correlated than strategies using say one minute bars to generate signals.

The movement in spreads is another issue to consider when trading with a broker who offers variable or changeable spreads. When using MT4, the strategy tester models opening and closing prices based on the last recorded spread. Backtests performed at two different times of day can produce significantly different results due to one backtest's assumed spread being much wider than the other.

My current strategy mainly uses daily charts to generate trading signals and the actual live results to date closely match a backtest over the same period so my backtest information is helpful to me in terms of providing rough guidance of past performance.

I think the key danger when using strategy testers is to mistakenly go down the road of over analysing and using the optimisation functions to fine tune strategy elements such as indicators in order to get to a desired profit or drawdown profile. Curve fitting a strategy in this way has personally led me to come up with a historically very profitable strategy only to find it quickly runs at a loss when forward testing.

In addition, it is a common approach for some traders to load a strategy with more and more filters so that the strategy rules become extremely complicated – to the point where only very precise market dynamics would result in success. My experience has led me to believe that the best strategy is often the most simplest.

3.3

FORWARD TESTING ON A DEMO ACCOUNT

As mentioned in the previous chapter, I do find backtesting useful but only to provide a rough guide in terms of performance potential. To trade a strategy live based only on backtest data is in my view a very dangerous thing to do. The next step I always take in evaluating a new strategy is to perform a period of forward testing on a demo account. This is so I can start to see how trading signals are generated using a simulated live trading environment and whether my Expert Advisor coding is being followed with expected results. It's a great risk free way to test the performance and check the coding accuracy.

The big caveat here is that demo account trading can again be significantly different to live trading so I always consider this type of trading as a guide only. This is because the demo account can fill trades without any issues of delay, price slippage etc.

From an emotional perspective, I have learnt to avoid getting impatient and make sure I thoroughly forward test my strategies before even considering going live.

3.4

GOING LIVE

When I have reached the point of switching my strategy on in live trading, I scrutinise every aspect of my system set-up and then check each individual market position being opened and closed very carefully. I monitor each position to ensure my strategy rules are being executed as I expect. I also regularly monitor my MT4 trading session, the VPS itself and all alerts I have set-up.

When trading live, real money is at risk and I always keep in mind that if something fails in my set-up, losses can mount up very quickly. To minimise any downtime, I ensure I have all the relevant support numbers with me in case of emergency e.g. I may decide to contact my broker to check or close a position if I'm unable to access my VPS for a long period of time.

3·5

LOT SIZE

I always use the lowest lot size possible when switching my live trading on, no matter how high my equity balance is. I consider the early part of my live trading as an extension of the testing period so that I am confident everything is working in line with my expectations before risking more of my capital.

Once I have analysed numerous live trades and have confirmed my strategy is being followed correctly and all systems are functioning as they should, I then consider the size of lot I actually wish to trade on each position.

My personal approach to determining lot sizes is to use position sizing by using a calculation of my equity. This calculation is something that can actually be coded in an Expert Advisor so I don't need to constantly monitor and amend lot sizes in my strategy coding as and when my equity fluctuates up and down.

The code I include in my Expert Advisor to calculate lot sizes automatically is as follows:

```
double My_Lots = NormalizeDouble
((AccountFreeMargin() * 3/10000),1);
```

The name 'My_Lots' can be named anything you wish but it must be referenced wherever the number of lots are required in the order sending code lines throughout the Expert Advisor.

The example code above will trade £3 per point if equity is £10,000 or £0.30 per point if equity is £1000. Before using something like this, ensure you understand how the lot sizes are being rounded as equity changes. I use the strategy tester to start investigating things like this.

3.6

MONEY MANAGEMENT

Some traders argue that money management is the most critical component of any successful trading plan and is something many traders overlook – at the expense of their capital. I certainly feel it is one of the most important roles when trading because if you get this wrong, you can be out of the game in no time.

As mentioned in the previous chapter, I prefer to use position sizing practices for determining lot size. In addition I use stops that aren't too close to the market i.e. so I don't get stopped out from normal market fluctuations.

My Expert Advisors actively monitor for my stop levels as opposed to actually placing a stop order in the market. The main reason I manage stops this way is because if my strategy has closed say a long position, I don't want another long position being opened in the same day. Coded stop monitoring was the only way I could ensure my strategy was executed in line with this number of trades limit per day rule I have set.

This coded method of placing stops is also something you may want to consider if you want to prevent falling foul of 'stop hunting' if you feel your broker does this. Of course if you truly believe they practice this technique, it may be time to switch brokers!

I don't use defined profit target amounts in my current strategy as I like my profits to run with the prevailing trend. I instead use a rule in my Expert Advisor to close the position when the market has reversed and breached say the closing level market price of the last couple of days.

So to summarize, as well as protecting against excessive downside risk of my equity on any given trade, my position sizing rules should mean my account gradually grows over time even if the average points won and lost were to remain consistent (assuming my win/loss ratio is positive).

PART FOUR

PROBLEMS THAT SOMETIMES OCCUR

Running my trading strategy is not always plain sailing and you should always be mindful of the fact that using a set-up such as mine is reliant on several systems all simultaneously working correctly.

The ultimate situation system wise is for all of the following resources I use in my toolkit to be online and functioning efficiently with no delays:

- VPS
- Windows Server 2008 on my VPS
- MT4 terminal
- Broker connection
- Expert Advisors
- MT4 email alerts
- TSMobiles application for remote access
- RDP and Wysecloud applications
- Monitis server monitoring alerts

A problem with any one of these systems may or may not affect the actual running of my strategy. At the very least, it will probably cause some kind of distraction which isn't ideal at the best of times let alone when busy at work.

Before implementing an automatic trading strategy in a set-up such as mine, it is important to consider the type of problems that can and do occur and have in mind a plan of action to deal with each of them.

Problems I have experienced along the way include the following...

4.1

PROBLEMS WITH THE EXPERT ADVISOR

An Expert Advisor is written code which details a set of instructions for the MT4 terminal to follow therefore one error in this code can cause unexpected problems when running the strategy on a chart. On occasion in the past I have been absolutely sure that my Expert Advisor was error free and ready to trade for real only to find a problem days or even weeks later. It is crucial to fully test your new Expert Advisor thoroughly over a period of time.

An initial assessment using historic data and then a forward test on a demo account should in my opinion be followed by live trading with the lowest lot size possible. Whilst trading live, the early trades should be carefully monitored to ensure the open and close signals are working in line with the strategy rules together with checks on how each order is filled e.g. are the slippage settings high enough to provide more assurance that a requested order will be filled.

Resources are commonplace on the internet that enable more robust coding of Expert Advisor's – for example if you are looking for a more robust order filling set of instructions, you may want to consider searching the internet for something like **"OrderReliable.mqh"**. This is a free Expert Advisor I use which makes fresh attempts on a loop to fill an order that wasn't filled previously due to an error e.g. the server or broker was busy at the time.

I've found this type of error handling can be especially effective when an order is being filled in the very first minute of the market open which is when my brokers systems are waking up with the day's first set of ticks for my chosen markets.

Again, with any form of coding make sure you thoroughly test it before even thinking of going live.

4.2

VPS DOWNTIME

When researching which VPS provider to use, you may want to assess factors such as cost, customer support levels, whether they offer a free trial period, and claimed server uptime promises or guarantees. Also check if there are scheduled updates that may affect the uptime of the VPS and whether these timed events coincide to market open times.

I have had only a few occasions of my VPS going down in the past year and the downtime has been pretty minimal so my trading has been largely unaffected.

It is however always a major concern if the VPS stops operating correctly as the trading connection to the broker ultimately stops. I believe one of the most useful tools in my set-up is the problem alerts provided by Monitis – as my server is monitored every minute, I can be very quickly informed of a problem and can react accordingly.

At the time of writing this book, I have actually experienced several downtime alerts with my relatively new VPS provider over a period of a couple of days. These were blips and only lasted a few seconds but were still a big concern.

After investigation, the VPS support team confirmed that the problem was due to a time syncing problem between my VPS and the main server. The technical engineers have now amended their system time synchronisation processes to refresh on an hourly basis and I haven't had a problem like it since. This is perhaps something to check with your VPS technical support team as any short term disconnection can affect the trading platform session's stability and running of a strategy.

As a VPS is a slice of a server and therefore shares a server with other VPS users, I am considering at some point switching my set-up to a dedicated server solution. A dedicated server will usually cost more each month however I like the fact that no-one else will share the resources on the server and this should reduce the risks of downtime following spikes in traffic or incidents of hacking attacks (rare occurrences it must be said but events that can certainly take a VPS offline).

If you need to switch VPS providers and don't wish to use their migration services to transfer all your data, you can use a large file and directory transfer service.

I have recently switched VPS providers and used Pando to transfer my platform files (including history data, Expert Advisor files etc.). I liked

Pando's solution as it was simply a case of installing their application on both VPS's and then using my email address to effectively send and receive the files I needed without having to use attachments.

4.3

MT4 DISCONNECTIONS

Unfortunately I haven't yet come across a broker that has been able to maintain 100% connectivity to their platform. Each platform I have used has at some point encountered a dropped connection which is obviously a concern at the time - especially if you have a live position open.

Thankfully I have found that MT4 disconnections with my broker occur infrequently and the downtime on each occasion is usually minimal and normally lasts just a few seconds.

4.4

EMAIL/SMS ALERTS AND REMOTE TOOLS

As well as solid system connections, I am also reliant on alerts informing me what's going on in terms of trade signals and downtime situations and also the remote tools I use to access my VPS. I have had frustrating situations of a failure of one of these tools when I've needed it the most. Sometimes I have had an email alerting me to a new trade signal but couldn't access my VPS on my Smartphone as data coverage was limited or non existent.

I have also had situations where I've accessed my VPS on one of my periodic monitoring checks only to find a position has been opened or closed without my knowledge – this was due to a delay in the push email system.

With regards to the systems I use in my set-up, there is inherently a risk of a trade not being filled without my knowledge for a period of time - this may exacerbate a loss (or indeed profit) on an open position. For this reason, I trade lot sizes that are relatively low risk when taking my equity into account. I also view my trading as a business as I am playing with real money here, so I will never just assume everything is working correctly. I check each and every trade to make sure nothing surprising has happened.

4·5

TRADING PSYCHOLOGY

Assuming your system set-up is operational and functioning as it should, let's now consider some of the emotions involved when running a strategy for real.

A strategy that makes money over time will most likely still encounter periods of drawdown of the account equity. Fluctuating market dynamics can provide false signals for extended periods of time meaning you could experience weeks or even months of losses.

Once you've finished the technical aspects of establishing your complete automated trading set-up and have been trading live for a while, you may find yourself experiencing emotional phases such as stress, impatience, greed and boredom. You may feel inclined to manually override your strategy settings as you feel it's not quite working out or you may find yourself wanting to tweak the settings due to a string of losing trades.

I've watched a trade go to within a few points of its stop level only to see the market reverse and switch the position to a winning one so I know it's a bad idea to fear the worst and intervene. Of course the opposite has also happened which can be difficult to deal with the first few times.

Personally I believe in my strategy and therefore stick with the rules religiously however there may come a point where the strategy is just not that effective any more. I will have to decide when the best time is to switch it off or place it on hold.

Some people argue the biggest factor that will determine whether a trader is profitable is whether that trader can deal with the psychological factors and strict trading discipline needed. I try to keep my emotions steady, regardless of whether the last trade won or lost. I am by nature quite impatient; however I don't risk more than a constant low percentage of my equity as I want to stay in the game and progress steadily.

4.6

EVENTS NEEDING A MANUAL INTERVENTION

Even as I rigidly stick to my strategy rules, I keep in mind there are periods when I may need to close a position early or switch off my automated trading altogether.

I never trade when I'm on an extended holiday as for me personally, not only is my holiday a time to relax, but I perceive the risk of managing my set-up too high especially if I am holidaying overseas. The markets have been around for a very long time and they are sure to be around for a good while yet so I don't feel the need to somehow find a way to trade every single possible day of my holiday duration.

I also keep a check on whether public holidays may mean my broker will close my traded markets early in the day or if the trading week is shorter than normal. I have also updated my own calendar with the public holidays that may affect my trading.

4·7

MISCONCEPTION OF AUTO TRADING

I believe it would be very unwise to fall into the mindset that automated trading can simply be switched on and left to its own devices. Too many things can go wrong so I am always monitoring my set-up and checking that each trade is working as it should.

Consider this - if a problem occurred which prevented one of my trades closing and I ended up making an unexpected additional profit of say 50 points, would I be happy? Not at all – sure I would be thankful it wasn't a losing trade but I would be immediately concerned with trying to figure out what went wrong and then look at ways to mitigate the risk of a repeat occurrence. In my view, anything that happens outside of my chosen strategy parameters is not welcome.

As previously mentioned, any downtime of the VPS, trading platform or a lost connection to the broker can all prevent the platform from opening a new or closing an old position.

Yes, it is fantastic that we now have these tools to enable us to trade all day every day, even with full time jobs, however I don't believe any automated set-up can be 100% trusted to get it right every time.

4.8

THE BIG PICTURE

It can be demoralizing when going through a period of losses and seeing accumulated profits start to fall away. That feeling of moving backwards in the goal of achieving trading success is disheartening.

One way I reassure myself is by fully understanding how my strategy may have performed in the past. Using backtest data, I can get a rough idea of how the profit profile may be over time by analysing the periods of drawdown in points terms. In my current strategy, there have been occasions over the years of several losing weeks in a row - sometimes as many as five or six. This puts things into perspective and I find this really helps my frame of mind and outlook when going through a bad patch.

When trading both the FTSE and DAX in my set-up, the losing periods sometimes collectively lost hundreds of points – however the winning weeks have more than compensated.

It is all too easy to focus on the upward trend of an historic graph showing profit over time, but the curve may not clearly illustrate those losing periods along the way.

The big picture is very important here – a robust strategy that is profitable over a long time period will undoubtedly suffer short term periods of decline.

PART FIVE

NEXT STEPS?

PART FIVE

I treat my trading as a fully fledged business therefore I have considered the future if and when my equity and lot sizes grow to much higher amounts.

When this happens, I believe the prudent thing to do is to look at ways of reducing the risk of losing any of my capital. One thing I will ensure is that my account balance with my broker stays within the regulators deposit guarantee limits.

The second area I will look at is the broker aspect itself. I envisage considering spreading the risk by using two different brokers to carry out my strategy.

In terms of my server set-up, I will review the existing system set-up and evaluate whether a second server is a good idea on spreading the risk. It will also be the time to consider other solutions offering dedicated servers and sophisticated redundancy systems if I feel my existing systems are lacking.

This is all assuming I continue to work full time. When my equity has grown to a high enough level, I may feel the time has come to leave my full time job and concentrate solely on my trading career whereby my whole toolkit may change.

CONCLUSION

I would like to finish by saying thank you for reading my book – I sincerely hope you have found the details of my toolkit useful. It has certainly taken me a long time to figure out a good set-up for my trading and I am optimistic this guide will save you many hours of work in figuring out which of the available tools out there will help your trading plan also run as smoothly as possible.

I wish you all the good fortune possible in your trading endeavours.

RESOURCES

You use these links at your own risk. The author of this book cannot be held responsible for their content or any problems arising from accessing these websites.

http://www.metaquotes.net

Visit for details of MT4 and Expert Advisors.

http://www.gkfx.co.uk

The broker I use for spread betting with the MT4 trading platform.

http://www.CloudNext.co.uk

My VPS provider.

http://www.rdmplus.com

The website for the TSMobiles mobile remote access tool. Shape Services is the organisation.

http://www.wyse.co.uk

The provider of the Wysecloud application I use to remotely access my VPS on my iPad.

http://portal.monitis.com

I use Monitis for my VPS monitoring and email alerts in case of downtime.

http://www.mt4i.com

The provider of the MT4 auto restart tool.

http://www.pando.com

The file sharing solution I used when switching VPS providers.

http://sufx.core.t3-ism.net/ ExpertAdvisorBuilder

An online Expert Advisor builder.

ABOUT THE AUTHOR

The author is a qualified Management Accountant (ACMA, CGMA) who is striving to break free from working for someone else.

This is the author's first printed publication after releasing the same title as an eBook.